FREELANCING 101

"You don't dream and wait for it to happen; you do something to make it real, you hustle."

BY *ATAHAN ASLAN*

CONTENTS

INTRODUCTION

In our new social world, where everyone uses social media or websites nearly in every aspect of life, the things we use are not only limited by social media. People are using the internet more and more to get their work done by people who have the necessary skills to do it. This was there all along in our world, but it was made via companies or even groups that have the proper license to do it. But in our modern world, this is not the case anymore. Something called **"freelancing"** has been developed over the past decades, and now it is capturing every aspect of getting a job done.

What is freelancing? Freelancing is the job of getting something done without a license or not committed to a particular company. People who do freelancing is called **freelancer.** Freelancers are people who are self-employed and generally work from home and generate the work which is wanted by people remotely with a lower price compared to companies or employees who are committed to a workplace or an employer. **But,** freelancers sometimes can be hired by companies when their workers aren't enough to cover their job or to cut expenses and not to pay any wage because freelancers don't get a wage even if they are working for a company, they get their money from the customer's job's commission. They just represent the company.

Now, in this book, you will read the **story of a young freelancer** and see the necessary aspects of what is needed to **become a freelancer, what to do, where to go** and **which skills** to **develop,** and **how to find customers**. This all comes from the experience which I have been doing. This will mainly cover the **translation** freelancing, but you will see the big picture in all.

CHAPTER I

BEGINNINGS ARE ALWAYS HARD

You are on the verge of starting something, something that may change your life. You are full of life, full of excitement about the thing you are going to do. You are still thinking to yourself, what am I going to do? How am I going to start all this? It's actually pretty easy but also complicated. The most important things are to be consistent with your work and be patient with your development. Always fight your way out; never give up. When starting freelancing, no matter what you are going to do as a freelancer, there are some basic rules you need to follow. Those rules are;

- Find what you like to do.
- Try to find something that has a big market.

- Take a step and research what you are going to do.
- Have some knowledge about your market and your area.
- Try hard and develop what you have chosen.
- Meet with people.
- Market yourself.
- Hustle every day and get better.
- Become successful.

Now, these points might seem like nothing, might seem like everybody can say, but in the upcoming pages, I will be going deep about what they actually are about. You are going to learn the basics and also the mechanism of how freelancing works and what freelancers go through to become successful or make it a side-hustle job to earn some extra cash.

Half of the freelancers on the market have started this freelance journey thinking they could make this a side hustle and earn some money either to help their college expenses or to add even more to their 9-5 job. And the other half of the freelancers are doing this as a full-time job, and these people are so much, not a small number. I will also talk about full-time freelancing and freelancing as a side hustle job.

Both have their own advantages and disadvantages, and it is your call if you want to make it a side hustle or a full-time job. You are new, this is the beginning, and you came here to understand and learn what this "freelancing" thing is about.

But you also need to remember that freelancing, even though it seems easy and not time-consuming, it is not like that at all. It takes time, even when you are a pro, and you have to spend a lot of time regarding the job you do. And it is not easy because you are dealing with people. There are millions of people around the world, and there will also be people who are not kind and treat you like a piece of garbage. But don't worry, this is all fine. You will also learn how to deal with this. It is a long phase, as I said, and we will go through every single thing there is in the book.

FINDING A SKILL

About 5 or 6 years ago, I realized that I have a passion for learning languages. Back then, I didn't know any languages, including my own language. I didn't even know the rules for my language, but I didn't know this before I started to be a freelance translator. I started to learn English from scratch, I worked and studied very hard, and after around 7 or 8 months later, I managed to really understand the language and speak it with other people. It was time for me to do something with it. I started to search for opportunities I could do with this knowledge. I, then, came across about being a subtitle translator, and it intrigued me because back then, I was watching a lot of TV shows and movies, and translating the subtitles of the shows and the movies I have been watching or watched excited me and therefore I started to search about what can I do to learn it and start it as soon as possible. There weren't many sources about it, let alone being a translator but about being a freelancer—literally nothing. I didn't have anything or anyone in my hand to look up to. So I had to make my own guide and my own rules. Everything was just getting started.

So, I started to search. I found a website that people voluntarily translate subtitles and upload for people who want to watch it from torrent. I first learned the subtitle translating program, and after watching a couple of videos, I wanted to try it myself. I knew it wasn't going to be worthy even to read, let alone watch it. I translated a whole episode, which took me about 5 or 6 hours! I uploaded it, and of course, it got rejected. All that work **went for nothing**. I was furious but also kind of happy because I started something, found what I was going to do, and found my skill. Afterward, I tried a couple more shows, but only one of them got approved, but it was because there was no other translation, and my translation was marked **"very bad."** Think about the drama, right? But I didn't give up; I wanted to change the way I was working.

I found a website to translate subtitles, it was kind of a miracle that I got accepted, but I was going to translate them for free. They were going to make use of me by giving me not-so-watched shows and translating them for free, and I was going to make use of them by translating shows and learning how actually the translations work from feedback and from experience.

That's how you find the skill that you like to work on. In this story I gave you, I didn't look for it; it was right next to me all along. So figure out something that you like on a daily basis, but it doesn't have to be necessarily something that you do. It could be something you watch, write, or something else. Mine was something I was watching. I was watching a lot of TV shows back then, so it led me to be excited when I heard that I could translate the subtitles to the shows I have been watching. Think about the fun and the excitement. You could be famous one day because of the job you do. (I didn't become famous, but that's out of the picture.) I once had a friend who became a freelance writer because he needed money when he was studying and was a fan of writing stuff, so he turned it into something that pays off money. In other instances, most of my colleagues throughout my translator career were university students. They started this whole thing because they needed money for their education and realized that they have a particular skill in this and developed it, turning it into something worthy.

During one of my trips to Europe, I had to wait at the airport for my flight for about 4-5 hours. During that time, I met a man who was a freelancer and was working with his laptop during all that time; later on, I learned that he was a blog writing freelancer, and he has been writing something that his client gave to him. I wondered how he got into this freelancing job because writing blogs don't come naturally; you have to have some basic skills, or rather, you have to work on it for a very long time. He told me that one day when he was in school when he was around 16 years old, he had to write a couple of pages about something he wanted because of homework his teacher gave him. He ended up writing 20 pages. That's how he realized that he likes writing, and he has been writing ever since, but for the first couple of years he started to write things, it was for himself because he didn't know what freelancing was, he didn't earn money, or he didn't write for anybody else, he was just writing for nothing. But then he learned how freelancing works, how it is, and he jumps right onto it. And ever since, he has been writing blogs. He even wrote a book later on.

This is one of the purest examples you can get. After reading this book, you might realize that you actually like something to do, and you can focus on that. If you can't find or remember anything, do not be afraid, just think. Ideas are essential, and they won't come in just one night; it takes time. You'll have to think about it, think about the things you do on a daily basis, as I mentioned. For example, this guy and my story can be a case study for you. Thanks to one of my teachers at school, I realized that I actually like learning languages and doing something with them. And this guy I met realized it without even doing anything. Sometimes, it requires some luck; sometimes, it requires overthinking. Although your luck might have already come to you, you didn't realize it yet, think and realize it. If not, **create your own luck**. That's how it works in this business.

But, you have to remember that this part seems like it is easy to do, but it is not. It requires a bunch of thinking, patience, and a lot more things to cover, so if you are stuck at this level, don't be afraid; you will find something that attracts you; there is something you like. You are trying something new, and it is **not going to be an overnight success**. My overnight success took me two years.

So, all in all;

- Do not be afraid to take responsibility.
- Try to find things that attract you in your daily life. It could be reading news, which could lead you to be a proofreader; it could be writing or something else. Figure it out, but don't forget, this part is the hardest part of all.
- When you find your skill, do not engage quickly; absorb it, think about it.
- What you choose to do is not going to be an overnight success.
- This is just the beginning, be ready for a very long journey.

First Principle;

"Ideas don't come easily; you either have to think a lot or create your own luck."

LEARNING THE SKILL

When I finally got into a website where I could work without interruption from not sharing it because of rules and just doing my work, I worked hard and so much. I learned through experience, which, in many cases, is the best way to learn something. I translated a lot of TV shows there because I wanted to get better. I wanted to have experience and read some critics about my subtitle, which I read a lot.

The reason why I learned my skill **through experience** was because of the lack of source and because this skill is actually something you can't learn by reading or watching, but you need to work on it. And that is what I did. You have to understand that not everyone or every job or every skill requires the same attention. Some people want hugs, good words, or just being calm. It is the same with skills or jobs, too. Some skills require reading or watching in order to become better at it, whereas others require pure experience, getting into it and losing while doing it. You have to learn what you need to do in order to get better at the skill you have chosen.

When I first started studying at university, I wanted to learn more about what I wanted to do in the future. So, I used what I did before and wanted to get some experience. I wanted to do marketing in the future, so I needed to learn about marketing tools, how marketing works, etc. I searched a while on the internet and this time – Thank God- there were tons of sources that I could look up to. So I found an app where entrepreneurs were offering classes about marketing segments in return for something for their website or startups. It was a win-win situation. I was getting the experience I needed, and they were getting their job done for free.

Therefore, I signed up. I took the first step regarding the skill I wanted to learn. I found some entrepreneurs who were ready to give me info & experience in the marketing field. But I wasn't qualified enough for the job they wanted to, and **I got rejected**. It doesn't matter; I kept going on. I finally found someone who was ready to give me a job. He was an old man from the USA, and he wanted me to market his little website. And I did, we got some good results, and this was my first experience as a marketer.

On the way to learning the skill you have chosen, you have to remember that it is **not going to happen in a day**. It will take time. And, in my opinion, this is the **longest phase** of this. It will require you to be patient, work on it for a long time and act on it without stopping. You have to make it a habit because you are learning something new. Just like you can't learn math or physics over a night, you can't learn a skill that will make you earn money from it over a night. My phase of learning subtitle translations took me about **1 or 2 years**. Well, to be honest, in my case, you never stop learning. Languages are complicated things to work on and especially if it is something that you go very deep into the language(s). Not just one language, but at least two.

In another instance, the guy I talked about in the other chapter learned how to write with experience, too. He wasn't working with anyone; he was just writing and writing and writing. He kept going on. He read the things he wrote million times until he decided there was no mistake or there wasn't anything to fix. Learning something requires patience. You have to fail a lot. You have to get criticized. After he did this for a couple of years, he presented his works on his bio, his CV, and other places for employers to see. Thus, he immediately got offers because his works were really good and nearly without mistake, people thought he was a very experienced writer. But in reality, he was just getting started.

It takes 21 days to turn something you do into a habit. If you do something 21 days continuously without stopping every day, on the 22nd day, you feel the need to do that whatever it takes. So try to work on your skill every day, and after a while, you will realize that you made it a habit, something that is a part of you, like brushing your teeth before you go to bed or showering. It will become a part of your life. Just keep on doing it.

As you can see, this is a long phase, not like any other things I mentioned, or I will mention. This is only the beginning, and the hardest parts are always the beginnings. You have to be ready for failures, rejections, and many more bad things. The good things only will come in the late phases, just like everything else in life. Be patient. Fail. Lose. Only then will you be a successful freelancer. Use everything you have in your hand, search. Focus on it.

Second Principle;

"Be patient; find sources; if you can't find it, create sources on your own terms."

DEVELOPING THE SKILL

Now, everything was easier and smoother after I was finally able to translate like I wanted and get them uploaded to a website to see the critics and help me get better at it. Because people were watching it and then they were highlighting my bad translations to me, and since I was working for free, my boss wasn't saying anything because he knew I was new and he expected those things from me. After working there for about a couple of months, I realized that that place wasn't helping me too much because, except for the experience part, I wasn't getting to know anyone so that they could help me. I applied for another website, and it was pretty hyped at that time, and getting there would help me a lot, I thought. I am not exaggerating; I applied to the same website about **10 or 15 times and got rejected every time**. But on my last try, I got in. I was finally in, and there were tons of experienced translators in there that could help me.

But in there, I had to be more careful because every mistake I made was counting, and they weren't going to pity me because I was new. This was the big league. I had to play according to that. Contrary to what they wanted from me, I wasn't getting any money, so I figured since I was working really hard and trying my best, why wasn't I getting any money? Even though we had a deal that I was going to work for free, I wanted some money that would cover my expenses. They offered me something – which was insanely low – and I accepted it. I was finally **getting paid**! After one year and **tons of rejections**, I finally did it.

Now, this is the easy part. You chose your skill, you chose the area you are going to work in, you started to learn it, and you know the basics; you just have to develop it. Everything is going to be step by step, but you just passed the hardest parts; the rest will come like a piece of cake. When you started to learn the skill, you chose a path of learning that skill, but when you had enough of that and got everything you could, leave that and search for something else, but this time, it will be easier because you know what you are doing, you have experience. You just have to find some company or someone that would give you a job. Use the people you met when you started to learn the skill; they will help you a lot, don't underestimate those people's connections because they are just like you, and they are searching for a mentor.

On the path to developing your skill, you will get rejected a lot because you are new and you are not really good at what you are doing, you are making mistakes, you are seeking help from other sources, and maybe you are not very creative. Do not worry, everything will be fine but in your first years, read all the critics, don't feel bad, read them and learn every mistake you made. Change them, fix them and be better. You will see that everyone who criticized you or humiliated you will be proud of your work. Just hustle, don't care about other opinions, fight for your work, dreams, and the rest will come. These 3 phases are the phases in which you will be humiliated or get criticized too much because, as I said, you are new, and there will be people who don't want you to get better, or there will be people who are egomaniacs and instead of helping you, they will just humiliate you.

When I was traveling a couple of years ago, I met a woman in an airport in Italy, Milan. She was young, around my age, we started talking, and I then learned that she was working in a small town in Switzerland in an area from which she didn't graduate. I asked her, "how?" Because right now, I am in the same situation, I am studying something, and I want to be something else, she told me, "I don't know. It just came up to my head, and I realized that I'd have fun doing that. I searched a little bit online, and the next thing I knew, I was on YouTube, watching videos about it. I tried to learn it on and off throughout the years during my bachelor's and master. And I did learn it. Throughout my college years, I met with people, learned skills, and I got certificates from online courses. After that, finding a job in that area was easy because I knew what it was, how it was working out in the daily-life business."

This is the story tells a lot. She realized that she likes to do something; she chose it, learned it, and developed it through multiple things. Do not stick to only one thing. Meet people, watch videos, do something about it even if no one sees it or it doesn't get published, do it. And if you can, get online courses with certificates that actually certify you know this. This way, even without the experience, you will get what you want because you have tons of experience, and no one can't deny this. It is here; it is the truth; you know what it is, you know how it works.

Developing something, it doesn't matter if it is a skill or even a relationship with someone you met, requires attention; you have to make it your habit to work on it. Otherwise, if you don't do it every day and work really hard on it, it doesn't become a side hustle or a full-time job, it becomes a hobby that doesn't pay at all, and you can't get any better with it. I had a friend who studied photography in university and in photography you need to take a lot of photos in order to become good. When I first met him, he didn't know much about photography but later on, he studied hard, watched videos, learned how the machine he has works, and then he started to take photos and too many photos. I wasn't even able to see him for a whole year. During that year, he did so much that he opened a website to showcase his photos at the end of the year, which ended up well for him, getting a lot of customers.

This guy followed a pattern. A classic pattern which you should also think about following: at first, he didn't know anything about photography, but then he used the internet as a tool to get insight knowledge about the postures, tips and later he went on getting experience on the streets. This is what you should consider. That's how you develop something that you don't know anything about. You just have to work hard. Talent is not important, **and hard work passes talent when talent fails to work hard.**

Third Principle;

"Get stronger with every rejection you get."

FINDING CUSTOMERS

When I was working on the website that I applied for tons of times, there were some people who had connections with other people. Networking is the key when finding customers to work with. Because, when there are people in the middle who knows you and can connect you with employers, everything becomes much easier since they know you and can believe the words of their friends. A couple of years later, into working with the website I mentioned above, one of the translators who was really experienced in the field approached me with an offer. Guess what the offer was? Probably, for a freelance translator, it could be one of the peaks to reach to. The offer was to work for Netflix. I was really excited when I first heard about it, and I told him yes, I was interested. A couple of weeks later, he suggested me to his employer, and after a trial translation, I was in. I was going to work for Netflix. And I achieved this in approximately five years. Even though Netflix Turkey quit sending TV show subtitles to the companies and started to translate them within its own network, I was in for a moment. It was a half failure and half success.

What is important while doing is to keep meeting people and not letting them out of your hands. You'll always be in-crowd, you'll always be working with other people while doing your own job, you just have to keep your eyes open for every single opportunity and not reject it because it seems bad or small to you. You are small, too. You'll grow bigger by eating small things. That's how it works, even in games.

In my first year in college, I went abroad, to a place where I didn't know anyone. So I got to meet with people, a lot of people and when meeting people, you tend to say what you are doing besides your school especially if it is taking a lot of time of yours. So, I told this to a bunch of people, but my main purpose wasn't to brag about it; my main purpose was to find customers, networking, as to say. Tons of people heard this, but since I was only translating in one language pair, and Turkish is not one of the favorite languages in Europe, so I couldn't say it worked out perfectly, but one time, one of the people whom I mentioned I was a translator came to me asking that he has a friend in need of help. I didn't know who he was what I was going to do; I only knew that I was going to translate something from English to Turkish and vice versa. I accepted it without further questions. He was surprised when I accepted it without hearing the details about the job but didn't say anything.

Even though I didn't want to in the first place, because I didn't know where, how, who, I went there because I needed to do it in order to add that to my CV and at least get some other experience, it was a short chat translation between a real estate guy and a buyer. I didn't think of it as something small or something useless; I knew it was going to pay off in the future, which did and gave me another couple of jobs.

My point is that you can't know where the opportunity might come from. Be open to everything and market yourself. No one besides yourself will be marketing you to other people. You are your own marketing department, and you have to do it in style. Act accordingly.

There are some key points that you have to follow when you think that you met a potential customer or someone that could help you. And when you do these, it will help you to get them more quickly and easily than it ever was before. Before listing these things, you have to understand that finding a customer, aka networking, is not all about talking about your job. You are not going to talk about your job, if you do, that will bore the person, and you will end up not getting the job. If you meet that person in a meeting or somewhere else where you can talk face-to-face, just mention what you do and leave the rest to their mind. Here are things that you need to follow in order to at least get a good prosper of what it looks like to market yourself and how to act while meeting a potential customer.

- Just mention what you do, leave the rest.
- Tell the person about yourself, your ideals.
- Exaggerate yourself if necessary, like making up a story.
- Learn a little bit of marketing, at least get the principles of it.
- Market yourself in every situation, either bad or good.

- While introducing yourself, talk about the other person and how good his job or whatever he is doing is.

These are just simple and short explanations about what to do but think about these and do it in your own way; if you memorize a pattern and try to do it in every person you meet, that won't work. Figure it out yourself on the field.

Dealing with people is one of the hardest aspects of this job. It is actually the same with every job. If you are dealing with a human being, you have to be careful and also a professional if you are trying to sell something to them. Because every word you say is a weapon, you use against them. If you use your ammo wisely, in the end, you will get the win, but if you just shoot around everywhere without a proper plan and finish your ammo before hitting your enemy, you die. It is the same with selling. It does not matter whether you are selling a product or the job you do. Make a plan before you go out there. Your first plan won't work; in fact, your first couple of plans won't work. You need experience. Also, you need to be able to read the people. Now, this is hard because everyone has their own unique set of mind on how they act. But once you figure out what the person you are working or talking with wants in someone, you already won the battle before it even started.

There are tons of marketing courses/videos on the internet. There are even courses for that. You have to know what marketing is in order to attract people. This will also take time, but while learning it, this is something you can try out on the field even with a little knowledge. Just go out there, meet people, use your skills. You are new; you have the excitement, the passion, everything you need on your hands because you are trying something that you have never done before. You have to use this as a tool for yourself and power yourself.

Fourth Principle

"Everyone is a potential customer; act accordingly."

CHAPTER II

NETWORKING

You have learned the skill, you have mastered it, you have the experience, and you know people in your area because of the experience you got from the first time. Everything is good, settled, and jobs are coming (maybe not); the first penny was earned, you have achieved it. Now comes the other parts. Namely, networking. This is a crucial part actually because to network, you have to have the necessary means, which I mentioned in the first chapter. If you already did what I told you in the last section of the first chapter, you already know the basics about what should be done in order to network – to get to know people.

Although working with people is hard, you need to make it an easy task for you, like a daily job that you do in an orderly fashion. Start with your current employers. Case study them, their behaviors, what they want from an employee and especially how to act among them and how to sell something to them. Because, I mean, as you can see, this is the person type you can get along with. So, you don't have to kind of worry about them because you already have this type of person on your hands, work on the other types which you can't get along with.

Probably, along the way, you had some problems with people while trying to work for them. It could be either a time issue or the job you have given to them wasn't enough in their own aspect or something else something entirely stupid or a normal case. Think about those people and try to make a case study out of it. That's experience and a mistake; learn from it.

One time, I had a job with a guy whom I didn't know anything about. A friend of mine suggested me to him, and he had a job for me. And I said, okay, I can do it. He came to me and asked if I could make a try-out because he needed to be sure about it. I didn't want to do that because it is time-consuming, and I had already proved my point in my job, which my friend already knew. If you are referred to someone, you don't want to get an audition; you just want to do your work because you came from a reliable source. But I didn't want to say to his face that I didn't want to do an audition because if I did that, he would just cancel the job. He seemed someone like that. So I needed to use another way of saying that I don't want to do a try-out. So instead of saying in a furious way, I told him that, of course, I could do an audition, but since I got referred here by a friend of ours, I didn't think an audition was needed because I thought he trusted him and asking an audition means you don't trust him and think about what our friend will think when he hears you did an audition to a person he referred? It won't be good for me, either.

In this case, I played to his character, and sometimes you need to do this. After I told him this, he didn't give me a try-out saying I was right. Dealing with people isn't easy; you learn it through time, but also it is complicated. The human brain is not only one kind. It has a variety of states of mind that you need to experience through and learn. You can't learn this with videos, books, or any other stuff. You have to experience it.

Some of has already have this kind of skill because of our life experiences, but some of us don't have that. So, when you meet with someone new or even with your friends, look at how they behave, how they react when you say something, and try to make a concept out of all this.

I will try to cover the basic things of networking, where to get to know people, how to act, and many more. Here is a shortlist of what we will see through this chapter;

- How to interact with people?
- What are the websites you can check into?
- How to act around potential customers?

These are the basic principles of networking. As in other chapters, they may seem easy to do, but when you go into the very deep of it, you see how it is different in the world itself.

FIRST PHASES

Like every step of every new thing, networking is hard, too. Networking has always been one of the hardest things to do, especially if you are trying to do the networking on social media, even though we live in a world where everything runs on social media through ads, posts, or even stories. Most of the companies succeed through social media, but, nevertheless, a lot of business, companies, and freelancers loses because of social media. There are a lot of opportunities and people who can outsource and outperform you. You have to perform your best asset in order to have a good networking environment and get the people to work with you.

A couple of years back, when I was really into freelancing and doing something with it, one night when I was scrolling through for jobs on the internet, an idea came up to my head which sounded crazy at first, but everything sounds crazy when you first hear them, right? Facebook was built with a man called Mark Zuckerberg buying a domain for 100 dollars and getting ads to support it without anything. So, the idea that came up to me was blogging. Blogging might seem easy from the outside; I mean, you are writing something after all, how hard could it be to do that sh*t? That's what I thought and started to search through. It is not as easy as it seems, believe me. I was looking and looking, and the only thing I saw was a lot of opportunities that I could use. I started to think about how to get better at writing because I needed some kind of expertise and some proof that I am actually good at it. I tried to write some stuff which I did, and I thought it ended up pretty good. But it turned out they actually weren't. I didn't get any jobs through websites. I wanted to try to do some networking on Facebook, Twitter, or some other social media, and I ended up posting posts on Facebook groups for freelancers hoping to get something out of them. Eventually, I did. I did a job for someone, and then a couple of weeks later, she told me there was a job opportunity for me to do for one of her friends. And afterward, he needed something else, etc.

That's how networking works. You meet and do some work for them, and in the end, if they really like what you did, they offer you to other friends they know who are in need of a freelancer. And afterward, when you really have the environment which we call "network" enough, you will get through the day and do a lot of jobs.

In other instances, when you are really good at what you do, you don't sometimes necessarily do something to have a good network. Because success spreads quickly. So you kind of have two options on this, and I do not prefer the latter. It is too risky, and to become that good at something, requires years, and when you are good like that, you have some really solid background, and the people whom you worked with already know your name. So, the latter is a risky and a very hard one. That one could be done only on the level on which you became professional.

Networking is also a very fragile thing to do because every single mistake you make on your jobs or even on the things you see counts. If the person you are working for is really careful about every single detail on the job, probably, when you make a mistake that he/she sees, that would be the end of your working relationship. So you have to revise the things you do tons of times to avoid big or even small mistakes that will cause scenery. Of course, this kind of revision only applies when you are just new to this and trying to prove yourself. When you make no mistakes in your early jobs, the rest will come like a piece of cake.

When doing your job, it is also important to be careful about the time. Customers generally give you a day or a time to give the job at the latest at that date. This is very crucial because the date they give is generally is the date on which they don't want it. Let's say that the customer wanted you to give the job in 5 days' time. You are relaxed because you have five more days to complete this job, so you want to take it slow so that you can do it solid and without mistake. Well, I am afraid to say, but this is one of the mistakes you make. When you get a job, start working on it immediately and try to finish it as soon as possible because when you deliver the job before the given date, even if your job has some mistakes on it, delivering it earlier than planned will give you credit so that the employer won't say much about those mistakes because they are kind of astonished from the way you handled the job so quickly!

One time, I had a customer, and the job he gave me was really long. I mean, he wanted me to give the job in 3 days which was impossible to do, but I was new at it, and I didn't want to blow off my first chance by asking to make the delivery date longer. I had to do it somehow, and I had no idea about how to do it. I tried my best only to realize that I couldn't do this in 3 days because it was the last day and I had approximately more than 30% to do. I asked for a longer period of time to deliver the job. He said it was okay, but it was clear that he wasn't happy with that. After I delivered that job to him, it was really hard to get a new job from him or around the people who knew him.

It is hard to deal with people, especially when you are trying to make something new out of nothing. Everyone will find a mistake in what you did because nothing is perfect, but you have to try to be close to perfect on the jobs you do because otherwise, you'll end up not getting the job. People who give the jobs are crazy, not lying. You are going to have to be crazy as well with them. I became one, and it worked out!

A couple of years back, I had a friend who had been doing freelancing on translations for about ten years approximately, and he was an experienced and well-known translator in my country, Turkey. He was taking jobs without even doing anything; jobs were coming to him.

Once, he told me a story where one of his employers gave him a job, and then after a couple of days later, he canceled the job even though my friend did nearly half of it, and he didn't get any payment out of it. He never worked with his friend who offered him. When you are that experienced and good, you have the chance to reject the employers. You won't be chosen; you will choose yourself.

Fifth Principle;

"Learn your audience, and if they are crazy, become crazy with them; if they are calm, be calm with them."

WHERE TO NETWORK?

Now, we have talked about networking, how to find people, and a lot more things. But **where** are we exactly going to find these people? Are we going to attend film galas? –Of course not- or are we going to go out and just meet people? Like I mentioned in the introduction part of the book, we live in a society where everything works through social media or the internet. We are going to use this as our networking tool. There are a variety of websites that will help you to find the customers and the networking you are looking for. I will give you a few websites to find potential customers or at least to meet with people. Some of these websites are known throughout the world, but I will give you the necessary information on how to do it. And some of these are probably you heard but don't know anything about it. I will teach it to you.

Facebook. Okay, let's start off easy. I know, I know, you know this website, why would I even write this down here? There is a reason for that. If you know how to use this worldwide, well-known website, it will be a great weapon for you to network. Facebook has a lot of options to cover. The first one is groups. There are groups for freelancers of which thousands of people are a member. In my opinion, this is not a good call because thousands of people are fighting to get one single job in a weird way in comments. The second option you can use is the ads. This requires some money, but since Facebook allows you to set your own budget, you can even advertise for five bucks. There are a lot of videos to teach you this. Give out an ad; this will show people that you care about your job, and spending on your job makes it look like you are actually earning out of it so you can spend on advertising it.

Instagram. This is one of the easy ones but also efficient ones, too. Use this to open up a page for yourself, for your jobs, and advertise it throughout Instagram. Instagram has the same advertising options as Facebook. Set your budget, let it go to the wilderness, and wait for people to come. Instagram is actually used more than Facebook, so try maybe using this on a continuous basis. This app offers way more than you actually think. Its advertising ways and how much you can achieve with such little money are so underrated. For under ten bucks, you will get way more than you actually wanted. Try it out; 10 bucks won't make you any poorer.

Upwork. That's the stuff. Here are the actual websites I have been talking about. Upwork is a website where freelancers can sign up and offer their expertise in an area or areas, and people can use the website for the expertise they are looking for. Upwork is the most used freelancing website on the web. So maybe try starting from here, sign up, add some experience, write down your expertise but when writing down stuff about yourself, you have to exaggerate yourself and market yourself in a way people can't reject. This website actually works in a different way. Buyers (people who need the job) opens up an ad on the website, and the freelancers can apply for it. And the buyer chooses the best candidate among them. You write notes; you give samples from your works and many more when applying for a job. But this website requires some time to spend because there are tons of freelancers, and they easily outscore you when you apply for a job. So maybe try and spend a little bit more time on this website and apply as much as you can. And what happens when the buyer chooses to give the job to you? He contacts you through Upwork's messaging system, and you come to a conclusion. You can choose whether to get the payment in one or split throughout the work. You can discuss this, and the payments are secured; if anything occurs, you can just contact Upwork, and they will resolve it for you. Yet, do not forget, it is important to make every chat on Upwork but not on other websites like Skype or something else.

Fiverr. This is one of the widely used freelancing websites as well. And in my opinion, this works a little bit easy for beginners because in this one, the system is a bit different, and it makes it easier to get jobs. In this one, you are the one who opens up an ad for the expertise you offer. So let's say you are a content writer and you want to work. You open up a job (It's called gig on the website) and talk about you, your job, and what you can offer. You can also choose to have three different packages on the job, like on Netflix. You can make a basic, normal and a premium one which everything varies from price to the delivery time and I think this is a great idea because you can arrange the word section saying that until this word count, I'll charge you this much and after this, you have to give this much. It is pretty convenient. But you can always try both websites. Because in this one, you just open the gig and wait for the employers to contact you, not the otherwise. In Upwork, it is the exact opposite. You apply for jobs and wait for an answer from the employer. So, use both; you won't use a lot of time on Fiverr because you just open a gig, leave the rest.

Guru. I didn't use this one so much, but I know the basics and how it works. It is similar to Fiverr. You post a job, and then you wait for employers to contact you. It doesn't offer as much as Fiverr when it comes to opportunities, but it is worth trying. Make sure that you open up an account, set everything up, and just occasionally use it even though it seems like it is empty because you never know when the opportunity will hit you.

Freelancer. This is one of the best freelancing websites, too. It has a lot to offer for both freelancers and for the people who are looking for a freelancer. You can use this one since its system is completely different from those I mentioned above. This website's freelancing system works on bidding. The employer opens up a job with a set price, and the freelancers start to bid on the job. But don't make a mistake by thinking this is a normal bid. Everyone makes their own different bids with different prices, different promised days of deliveries and etc. And looking at all this, the employer chooses among the candidates who bid on the job. The employer generally sets an amount with minimum and maximum input. Let's say you are an employer, and you need a logo to be designed; you open a job on this website, you write down the details of the job, you choose a budget, and let the freelancers make their bids on the job. Among the freelancers, you look at their offers, their promised days of deliveries, what they have written about them, their experiences and many more things and you choose it is according to that. This website also has premium features too. Like if you pay an amount monthly for premium, your bids stay up on the employer's list, you get more things to find jobs easier and many more, but I don't recommend this if you are good enough you will be able to find a job easily without spending money on a silly thing like this.

These are the basic websites to cover when looking to network. But, do not forget that you can network anywhere on social media. In my opinion, social media pages like Facebook, Instagram, and maybe even Twitter works better than any other freelancing website. Because in this websites you can find a variety of people who are in need or even thinking about giving a job to a freelancer. The thing about these social media pages is that you have to market yourself in a way no one else does, and for this, you need good branding. Therefore, the next chapter will be about how to create a strong brand and how to apply and market it throughout social media.

Sixth Principle

"Doesn't matter where you network as long as you can market yourself."

CHAPTER III

BRANDING YOURSELF

I have been going on about marketing yourself, marketing yourself, and many more. What is this about? How do you market yourself, and how do you achieve the trust that the employer is waiting for you? For that, it might sound like you need some marketing knowledge, but you don't need that. I will go through the steps one by one to teach you. You actually just need the basics of this, so I will try to teach you all of them. It is actually simple. Think about Nike. Go to a Nike store, whether small or not, take a look at the shirts or sweaters. You just see a normal black sweater but with a tiny Nike logo on the corner of it. You look at the price, and it is something like 100 bucks. But the sweater itself is actually a black sweater which you can find in where you want for less than 15 bucks. This is called branding. If you have the brand, the name, you can put the price as much as you want. But to do that, you need to do a good job and do some marketing. This thing is the same with Adidas, Puma, Apple, Samsung, and many more. Branding is important!

How did Nike or Adidas, or Apple achieve this branding thing? Before we start, that is what we need to learn. Did they spend hundreds of millions on marketing? When they first began, of course, no. They made a difference with their product's quality. This is your way of branding comes in. You are not going to spend a lot of money on marketing, and you are going to spend your time on doing a quality job.

I know what you might think. What does Apple have to do with any of this? It actually does, as I mentioned. Part of being a freelancer comes from how to market yourself. Well, you are going to market yourself with your job, of course, but how do you market your job? All those questions are the key to this chapter. You will learn it in this chapter.

MAKE YOURSELF THE BRAND

Congratulations. You took the first step regarding branding yourself. You have come this far, and so far, you know how to start freelancing, how to choose & develop your skill, and how to network your job to the customer who is in need of help. But now, you have to expand yourself wider. On the way to the branding, the essential thing is if you are working on your own to make your name the brand. Maybe create a website, or even give ads on Instagram on your name, showcasing your jobs, and after this moment, things become broader since you are not looking for a job; you are looking to expand your name. In this scenario, this branding is optional; not everyone necessarily does this because it actually means that you are stepping out of what you did and you are expanding to make it something more, which will go further beyond. But, I do recommend doing this if you have been doing it for a while and you wish to expand your business.

Sometimes, when you actually brand yourself in a great way, even when your name appears somewhere, the price and the quality go up. There was a translator once who was really popular in Turkey, he was really good at what he was doing, not going to lie and every product he translated in Turkey was becoming a show that people were watching because he was very well known thanks to his work. He was just a translator who was doing free translations on a voluntary website, but after he got well-known, he started to give consultations to websites, and he was making quality control for translators at one point. It is actually incredible how he got that far. He then translated for several television channels and many more.

That's what branding gives you, the opportunity to expand your business. You can do a lot more than what you were doing because people know that you actually are good at what you are doing, and you can check other people's work, you can give ideas to employers, other freelancers, and many more. You can even set up a course for people to learn it from. Of course, with the price tag on it.

After I was finally good at what I was doing, and after years of chasing jobs, I was, after all, on a website which was good and solid, and I wasn't looking for any jobs, but since I was into the job for a long time and proved myself, time-to-time I had job offers without even doing anything because people knew me and my work, so they were coming right to me when work was available.

This is the power of branding yourself. When something becomes a brand, and people knows it, it creates something that we call "brand loyalty," which results in people buying or using your stuff without thinking twice because they have the past experiences resulted as good in their opinion so, they think the next one will be the same or even better, so they buy it without thinking it. You have to create this. Share your jobs, become loyal so that people won't hesitate when they are going to give you a job. For example, I never hesitate when I buy the cereal I have been eating every morning for the past year because I have been already using it and I have a good experience, so when I am buying it, I just look at the name, and that's it. Before I had the cereal for the first time, a friend of mine offered it to me saying it was good, so I went to the store to check it out, I looked at it for a long time I checked other options, and it seemed better than the other ones, so I chose it, and I have been using it for over a year now. Before you earn the loyalty credit, you also have to make the first impression, too. First impressions last. This happens when you showcase your jobs in a good way because sometimes references aren't really enough to get people to work with you. I will also talk about how to make a good first impression and how to make it so good that it will last for a very long time.

So when branding yourself, there are several important factors to think about. But when doing all the things on the list below, don't do it too much; too much will turn into an idea of a "crazy person." Don't be that person.

Be the reasonable one, always. So here is the list of things you need to do when branding, and do not forget, this is not necessary in order to earn some money from this. This is for people who are thinking to go broader and wider in the case of working areas.

- Be the quality itself.
- Don't obey everything the employer asks. Challenge them; that's what they like.
- Focus on your loyal customers.
- Create customer loyalty.
- Be a brand.

These steps are the essentials. Focus on them; it will help you to grow as a brand on the open market of freelancers.

Seventh Principle;

"Without a brand, even the most quality item goes for pennies on the dollar."

FIRST IMPRESSIONS LASTS

Think about the first moment you saw or met with your boyfriend/girlfriend or your best friend or someone in your life that you care about or do work with. I am pretty sure that the moment you met, you liked them. You felt the connection between yourselves. Think about what would have happened if you didn't like them or had a fight, or didn't even talk? I'll tell you, you wouldn't meet and they wouldn't affect your lives this much. That's why first impressions are one of the most important things in our lives. Even with an item, if you like it, you take it. You have to be irresistible, and the best way to do that is to talk with people but in a fun way, not in a negative way. And how are you going to do that? I'll tell you how.

We all have our insecurities about something, and most of us have the insecurity to go and talk with someone we don't know. I know it isn't easy, but the thing is, you don't have to do this face-to-face since we are working on social media, well, actually you can also do it face-to-face, but it is going to be mostly on social media, so I am going to focus on that. Let's assume that you saw someone on social media or one of the freelancing websites I mentioned above. How are you going to talk to them? Are you just going to mention what you do and just tell them your price? Of course not! Don't ever, ever do that. You will never get the job. What you have to do is simple, find something in common with each other. It could be a sports team or something else. You don't even have to like or be a fan of what the other person likes, just have the information about it to talk it over for a while, that would be enough, or text them saying something about what they like, something they posted on their profiles is the biggest help! They will immediately answer because they like it and when someone who likes the same thing as them texts them, they are happy to talk or even help them – this one always work in every situation, try it- and then after talking for a while, just mention the work you do and say that you are looking for a job or whatever you are seeking from them. Since they like you from the beginning and assume they have connections, you will get a job soon.

Last year, I got into a movie subtitling website, and before I applied, I didn't have any experience with movie subtitling. Only TV shows, therefore, I didn't think I'd get in, but the employer e-mailed me asking a couple of questions, so I answered them, and one of the questions was what I was studying, and where and when I told him I study in abroad, he immediately started asking questions about which country, how is it, etc. I understood that this guy has or had been looking for ways to leave the country, and he couldn't. So, I told him every single detail, sometimes even exaggerated, and while saying all of that, I also said a bunch of things about how it helped me with my work, how it made me better, and in the end, we chatted for about solid 30 minutes, and after that, I got the job, and when I got it, he was really helping me, or he was making an exception when

I had extra classes or no time or something else. Not only did this connection help me to get the job, but also it helped me to bond with my boss.

That's how you do it; It doesn't have to be something you find; sometimes they ask questions about something you said, try to catch them and just move on from there, forget about the job for a couple of minutes and focus on the employer. You can talk about yourself all the time, but talking about another person is a one-time chance, and you have to use it very wisely. People always love people who care about them or their ideas or even what they say.

I had a calculus class in my first year of university, and I had no clue about how I was going to pass the class since my math skills were lower than a baby's writing skills. I thought about what I should do, and when I met the teacher, I realized he likes talking, just talking about approximately everything. After every class, I went to him with an excuse to ask a couple of questions, but every time we ended up talking for 30 minutes more or less. Every single time. He liked me, of course throughout the semester and in every subject or every single thing, he was coming to ask me if I understood it, yet, I had never mentioned him about my math skills, I didn't even say anything about whether I am good at math or not but he ended up asking me whether if I understood it or not about everything he tells in the class.

You can use this everywhere, but doing this thing on social media and getting a job from it is much easier than doing it in real life. Don't underestimate the power of talking with people. You have to like to interact with people as much as possible because interacting with people opens paths that you never think of even seeing. Also, don't forget that some people are just rude, I mean, when you try to talk to them they might not even say anything or might swear or something like that, don't lose your hope because he will regret not choosing you in the future when he sees you again, but you are not willing to work for him.

Moreover, when making the first impression, it is important to look like you don't need them; they need you. Like stand up, sit tight and talk with them with confidence and don't look like all bad and sad, that'll make them think that you have to get a job from them so that not only affects the rate of acceptance, it will also lower your job's price because you seem insecure about you and your job, causing people to think that you are new or bad at it. When someone offers a price or something about your job, kindly reject them, like saying, "I appreciate your offer/idea, but I have been working like that for a while now, and I am not thinking about changing it." Or something similar to this in a way where you don't hurt the person against you, but also you make them realize that you are special and you don't do this to everyone. You are special; act like one.

Eighth Principle;

"Act like you own the sector, not like a part of the sector."

STEAL THE LIGHT

Have you ever had the moment where when you were telling a story, and someone came in with something in their mind and started telling it and stole the light from you, causing your story to be unfinished? That's rude, right? You hate him for that, but there is nothing you can do about it because he already has the attention, and if you say something, you'll be the bad guy because you'll interrupt something exciting. Well, you kind of has to be that guy if you want to steal the light. It is not fun and not good, I know, but we have to do things we don't like in order to achieve what we want sometimes. Just go and talk to some employers, and if you see an employer about to hire someone for a job, tell them you'll do it for a lower price, and you have more experience than him and that you can prove it. Or play the moves I mentioned in the above chapter and use your skills to intimidate him. Sooner or later, you will steal the light, and you will get the job if you do it right.

You can also go out there and find a successful freelancer or a blogger (whatever you are doing) on social media like Instagram or Twitter and follow their followers with your social media account. People will look into your account, and if your account (as we call it, the brand) is better than the other one, they will follow you, and they will get in contact with you if a job is needed to be done. I know, I know, this is a badass or some slut move, but you have to understand that this is sometimes necessary, and it is one of the most efficient ways to get some followers into your blogging account or your social media.

Some of these things I mention especially having an Instagram or a Twitter account are about creating a brand phase. Marketing yourself in these places will make you look like a real professional, causing people to see that you actually care about your job and also, you can use Instagram to promote your jobs and share some of the jobs you made. It is also a great way to steal the light from other people by sending your works or showcasing them to other people.

The "Stealing the light" concept actually comes with its benefits, too. Sometimes, you end up doing so good jobs that people tend to realize that you are better than the person that you stole them from, which in return, it makes people suggest you to their friends, and it ends up with you getting way more jobs than you actually do cause you to have wider networking. But branding comes in here, especially when you start to have a bigger audience. Because when people talk about you, they are not going to talk about your look or your name; they are going to talk about your brand, your jobs. So, if you are planning on stealing the light, first make sure you have a solid brand in your hand so that when people see it, give them something to talk about other than shitty stuff like your look or your name. Give them your brand, and that way, stealing the light from other people becomes way easier than it actually is.

The toughest thing is to give better things than your colleague because if they have a wider audience than you have and you see their audience worth stealing, then that means they are actually good at their job and creating their brand. You have to make sure that you are better than him and not just in followers or in words, in action. Because actions speak louder than words. Do better jobs than your colleague and make him end up being under you in case of skills and reputation. It is vital to do that, don't forget, market your jobs, not yourself.

Ninth Principle

"Steal their light, not their jobs."

CHAPTER IV

ONE IS NEVER ENOUGH

Always living with this principle helps you a lot in life. Are you studying for math, and your hope is to pass? That is not enough; I hope to get more than a passing grade and work on something else; it will help you to focus on them more. This is the idea behind this. Let's say you have chosen to write a blog for a freelancing career, and you have been doing it for a while; you are good at it and earning money out of it. Don't stick with only blogging. There are tons of options you can do that your blogging career helps you out. Proofreading, content reading, or many other things will get you into these jobs if you are a blogger, for example. It necessarily doesn't have to be related to your area, but if it is something close to your area, it will be easier for you to get into it without any real experience.

I am both a translator and a blogger, for example. I have started translating years ago, and when I had enough experience, I wanted to diversify my skills because doing this will not only help me to earn more money but also it will help me to build my CV. Getting into blogging was rather easy for me because throughout the years while translating articles, subtitles, books, or other things helped me to discover how writing works and how the steps are really related to each other. Before I went to blogging, I wanted to write on some stuff, but I didn't know where to publish them or even what to do. So, this diversifying idea came up to me. What if I also become a blogger? What possibly could I lose? You don't lose; you earn. Experience, money, networking, people.

When you diversify, you tend to meet even more people, thus resulting in you getting jobs in your other area because you are a dual freelancer and can do two jobs at a time with much less money than paying two individual freelancers.

You have to think about every possible opportunity when it comes to diversifying. There are tons of possibilities that a freelancer can do. People pay tremendous amounts of money even for a little thing. Don't do just one or two maybe do more, things that are related to this field because for example, if you learn web designing, you learn coding and other stuff that is related to each other, so it becomes like a package just like when you learn Spanish; Italian, Portuguese and even French comes easy to learn.

I had a web designer freelancer friend, and he was designing websites along with designing logos, banners, photographs and he even got too far, and since he knows web designing, he knew a couple of things about websites itself, so he continued on that and learned the programming languages along with other things creating 3-4 jobs for himself. He ended up doing more than five freelancing jobs and earning tons of money. But he was working too much, needless to say, though since he liked it, he didn't care how much he worked. This is an important thing, too. Yes, learning them is possible but try learning things you enjoy doing, just like when you chose your first skill. Because if you don't like doing the thing you chose, you end up not doing them, and it will kill every joy you had, causing you to just stop chasing what you want eventually and stick up with just one job. So be careful when you are acting this way, it is tricky, and it never is easy to choose something else. Research it, try it out on your own before you start doing work for other people because you might end up hating it so much that you don't even want to finish the work you got from the employer.

Diversifying your talents and your time comes with disadvantages, too. You tend to spend more time on this side job; you become more active on freelancing agencies, websites, etc. It starts to consume more time than it did before. Make sure that you have enough time to do that because doing more than one job is really hard and time-consuming, like in every aspect of life. When you do something simultaneously, even on a daily basis, if you don't do things one at a time and do them at the same time, they seem harder, and you tend to make mistakes because you are tired, and your mind is literally split into two or more pieces.

How to maintain this? How is it really possible to do more than one freelancing job without losing control of our lives or even our jobs? It's not easy, I am telling you, but there is a way. You have to make a plan for every job you get, or if you are working with a company, make weekly plans and do them according to them. My advice is not to get into more than one or maybe two different job areas a day. Two is more than enough, don't go more than that you because you end up confusing what to do or even sometimes how to do it. In every way, you have to make a plan for the week or even for the next day. Without a plan, it is really easy to lose control of your job and your life, so start with making a plan. Even if you didn't start freelancing at all, still make plans because thinking about it, is it easier to write your daily or weekly tasks on a paper and cross them out one by one after you are done with them, or is it easier to just leave them in your mind where thousands of thoughts, ideas are passing through and leave them without writing and trying to think about the things you supposed to do and searching them within this crowded area? I think the first one is easier, right? So, be prepared for everything; plans are the best way to avoid losing.

Many freelancers work with the latter I mentioned. No plans, no ideas, just doing the job that is given and trying to rush them up to the deadline. Don't be like that; it not only causes you to lose but also causes you to be irregular with your deadlines, and people start not trusting you in any way.

One important aspect of diversifying your freelancing areas is to deliver your jobs way before the deadline. I already mentioned this, but the importance of this is much more when you diversify because you have more employers and more people trusting on you to deliver your jobs on time and if you deliver them before the deadline mentioned, although working with different areas, this will show your customer that you value your job and he might even consider doing another job in a different area. Value all of your jobs no matter how hard it is to control them in the way you want, but if you have a solid plan, well-made ideas, and good networking, this all should come easy, and even after a while, you can increase your prices without no one saying a thing because they know you are working so hard and you do a good job that you deserve a raise in your prices regardless of how it affects them. Being consistent is also one of the keys too. Always follow your plan, but you don't necessarily have to complete every single thing you wrote on your plan because it is generally not possible to finish them but at least try to achieve approximately %70 - %80. In time, you will realize that this percentage will go up, not down, and it will cause you to be more efficient and consistent.

So, efficiency, planning, and being constant are the key factors of diversifying your skill in freelancing. Freelancing is a hard concept to cover, and when you choose to make it harder than it is, you have to have some plan, idea, or the will to do all of it because it will consume all of your time and your mind, but while doing all of that, you have to like what you are doing. Otherwise, it will feel like hell. It will be wiser if you choose to diversify and put more effort into this. You are starting over just like in a game when you complete everything and start to do side quests. You have the basics, and you don't know anything about the new mission; you are going to learn it one by one again, you are going to consume time on them, be patient and elegant about it. Because if you don't do all of this, not doing just one step will put you behind a couple of dozen steps because every aspect of this, starting a new freelancing career, is hard, and there are some aspects that are needed to cover and follow.

Tenth Principle

"Diversifying is the key when it comes to doing more than you want."

CHAPTER V

ADVANTAGES AND DISADVANTAGES

Like everything we do in our life, freelancing has its own advantages and disadvantages, too. Some of these advantages cover up the disadvantages, some of the disadvantages actually don't cover the advantages. I am not going to lie, freelancing is mostly hard, but when you like it from the beginning, you get used to it quickly, and these hard things start to come as easy, and you start to have fun with it, you become crazy with it, in fact, you get so much crazy that sometimes you want to spend every minute in the day doing that work.

Having these advantages and disadvantages varies from sector to sector and from area to area in which you work. As a translator, when I was working for Netflix, it didn't have many disadvantages, I had 24 hours to translate the subtitle and give it to them, and I had the opportunity to check and correct my mistakes so that I won't end up getting fired. But after I quit Netflix and started to work on websites (which actually Netflix was just a phase, I mostly worked with websites), I didn't have as much time as Netflix to translate it; I had to translate them as soon as they aired on which country it was airing. Since it was generally the U.S, shows were generally aired at around 3 or 4 A.M. on Europe's time, so I had to wake up at 4 A.M. to start translating it, and I had to finish it within 2 to 3 hours depending on the show. Think about it, you wake up at 4 A.M., and you have to translate it without a break. But, after you are done with the show, you also have the day for yourself. As you can see, there are both advantages and disadvantages to this. I can count endless things about both of them, and we'll end up reading a thousand pages. But in the upcoming chapters, I will explain what the advantages and disadvantages are, how they work out and how you should act when you encounter a problem that causes a disadvantage and affects your life.

When I first started working, as I was translating for free and I was going to high school, I didn't have much time to get up early during the weekdays and translate something. I didn't know that I had to get up very early when I started to translate professionally. It was a bit of a shock. I remember that moment. I was working on my second website, and I finally had a big show to translate the next day; I was so excited. I prepared myself the night before and asked my boss when I should be expecting the subtitle because I generally started to translate subtitles – the earliest- at around 3 or 4 P.M. I thought something like that, but what answer do you think got from him? He said 4 A.M.! I was shocked for a while because I wasn't expecting it. Like, am I really going to wake up at 4 in the morning? At first, I thought I couldn't do it, but I was given the task once, I couldn't screw it up. I had to do it. So, I woke up at 4 A.M. the next morning; I did it. I was done by at around 7 A.M., so I slept back, and it was a really good sleep, not going to lie because I did my job, I achieved it now it was time to rest.

Sometimes, these things hit you unexpectedly in a way that might even hurt you, but you have to stay strong and fight it because that's when the real fun begins. You start to earn more after that because you got over that problem and now you can do that if someone asks you to do it again. It is as simple as that. You just have to do it without saying no. It's amazing how much it can change when you have the courage to do something you actually don't want to but deep down, you know it could change your life. Think about that and act like that. It will help you a lot, I promise. I will get into how to deal with them now in the next chapter.

Eleventh Principle

"Sometimes, things hit you from the angle where you don't look; you just have to surprise them/it by not getting affected by it."

ADVANTAGES

In freelancing, as I mentioned, these advantages and disadvantages can vary from job to job or sector to sector, but there are some general things that we can talk about to see if you can handle it. Of course, advantages are all the good things, but some advantages can turn into disadvantages if you don't handle them well. I will try to teach you how to handle them and how to change your perspective to not seeing all these advantages and disadvantages and to focus on your job.

The first advantage we can talk about is the one that most of the people choose this job for. When you are a freelancer, you don't have an office, and therefore you work from home. You don't have any working hours; you work whenever you wish, and you can have as many breaks as you want since no one is looking over your shoulder if you are doing your job or not as long as you can deliver the job on time. But as I said, these advantages can turn into disadvantages if you tend to use them in the wrong way, and I will mention all of these wrong ways in the upcoming chapter.

The second advantage we can talk about is that since on most of the jobs deadlines are long, or you have enough time to complete the job and control them; you can reduce the margin of error to nearly zero by reading or watching the job you did more than once, thus resulting in you having completed a perfect job that the employer will be satisfied with. When I was working with Netflix, I already mentioned that I had 24 hours to translate a subtitle. Translating a subtitle approximately takes 2 or 3 hours or maybe four if it is long. I was taking 10 or 11 hours to translate a subtitle and then taking 2-3 hours of watching it again and again, so I won't let any mistake come in the way of my job. I never got a warning about my job at all. So, while you are taking the time to finish the job, you also kind of need to plan ahead about everything, which I also mentioned. Use your advantages wisely!

The third one we can mention is something that most of us probably don't realize. When you are a freelancer, you have the right to choose whether you want to work for that employer or not. Generally, when you are talking business for the first time, employers tend to seem friendlier and more close to you, which, I am not going to lie here, most of them are pretty great employers, but there are several annoying people out there that you might encounter. I once had a boss, and he was really caring about every single word what other people about the work. The complaints were not really big; they were small things, or they were not even true at all, but still, he always wanted us (the translation team) to fix it, and when you tend to make those mistakes which some of them are not even real, he just fired them. You have to find the right people to work with. You don't have any boss; you can choose your own boss and work with the people you want. This is a big one, I am telling you. But you have to be careful when taking a job. Know your boss very well before you take a job from them because you might end up fighting all the time and having problems after the job.

The fourth one is actually something in the middle, but I call it an advantage. So, I have to say that not all jobs require this. Some of them are mostly in translation or any kind of works which is connected to other continent's time frame require this. When you are doing a job, sometimes, you have to get up early – very early – in order to fit yourself with the employer's wants. Sometimes, if you are working on a weekly basis where there is a constant job that is given, there are time frames in which you should do them. These time frames are generally for a whole day, but sometimes it requires getting up early in order to finish and sending it to the employer as early as you can so that the employer can use it fast. Now, getting up early is a problem for all of us, I know. Some of us are even happy that we don't have working hours or an office that we need to go to at 8 A.M. in the morning. But waking up early and finishing the job early gives you the whole day off which you can educate yourself or do more jobs or even just sleep. (I don't recommend sleeping) So, when you have a job like this, instead of thinking about how you are going to wake up and do it that early, think about what you will do throughout the day when you finish your job early in the morning. Turn disadvantages into advantages.

The other important advantage is that there is no limit to the money you can earn. You are not sticking to just one job.

You can do more than one; you can create multiple income streams, which will result in you getting paid way more than your 9-5 job. That is why there is a chapter called "One is never enough" in this book. If you are working, use your Saturdays and Sundays to learn a new skill and implement them; after a while, you'll realize that you set the limit on the money earned, not your boss. You can raise your wage whenever you want. Get more jobs to learn more skills. It's all up to you. This is a big advantage that you can use for very good things.

Another example of a "perfect" advantage is that you can raise your prices, and you can set your price to whichever you want. When you are working for a while, your skill gets valued, and you have the right to raise your prices. It is an open market; if you are good, you get to raise your price and get the double money you were getting last year. It's all about passion and networking. If you have been working with someone for over a year and they like your work and your personality, if you do not go over too much, you can raise your price however you want. It's your job, your fingers, use them. You always earn more; you never lose when it comes to pricing. Because people who like your job will give you the amount you set because they generally think you deserve it, and they have the resources to give the money since they are earning with it.

The last thing I want to talk about is that when you have work that you do employer by employer, not on a weekly basis, it is easier to prepare your schedule and therefore you have basically every moment off in your life. You can socialize (more networking!) and do whatever you want. But, I have to warn you, this is not basically an advantage when you go deeper into freelancing and start working on different projects with different employers and sectors, you start to have more jobs; thus, you start to have no time at all. Just because you don't have much work to do, doesn't necessarily mean that you can take all the week off and rest. There is no resting if you are new or in the middle; there is only hustle on your book. Be wise and clever, don't waste any of your time but occasionally, it is okay just to sit and chill with one of your off-days.

DISADVANTAGES

There are a lot of things to say when it comes to disadvantages. Everything has its own problems, and freelancing is just higher. But this doesn't change the fact that freelancing is way better than just having a 9-5 job and getting stuck to a chair all day long. You just have to suffer more at the beginning; the rest comes later. Half of the things I will mention here are not really that bad, but the other half might seem bad, and you might start re-thinking about this freelancing thing. But don't worry, I will tell every one of them with every detail and how to get over them easily without having or causing problems in your life. But even though I will mention how to get over it, do not forget that every beginning has its own different rough path, and getting that path is one of the hardest things in the world, be careful and be strong.

The first thing I will talk about is the first advantage I talked about in the previous chapter. Working from home, not having working hours, not necessarily having an office are good things, yes, but these all might turn into something bad if you don't know how to control yourself. If you can't control yourself when you have something to do, and you go watch Netflix or go out or sleep, it will affect your business very badly, and you might end up not doing any jobs and miss the deadlines. This is important; if you are thinking about becoming a freelancer and making this a full-time job, you have to have self-control in order to change the way how your life works. Do you want to work from home? You don't want to have working hours? That's all fine unless you can keep up with it. When you wake up at 8 A.M. in the morning, just getting back to sleep and thinking you will end up finishing the job that day is easy. If you just go back to sleep, you lose and will never be able to succeed in this business. This business, freelancing, requires patience, focus, and adaptation. The best way to get over this laziness and get some self-control is to push yourself to your limits. When you wake up in the morning at 7 or 8 A.M., you tend to go back to sleep if you are at home wandering around or working on the computer because the bed is right there; it is so easy to jump back in and start sleeping again, right? The best thing in the world, I don't disagree with that, but still, there are times that sleep is the worst thing in the world. Try to keep up with the pace and spend your day without touching the bed until you go back to sleep. This might be the key to your sleepiness. It's hard, yes, but you have to fight with it.

The second thing I will mention is something I mentioned throughout the book and touched upon in the previous chapter. Waking up early in your routine. This doesn't apply to every single job there is on the freelancing market, but still, there are some jobs that require this. Sometimes, you have to wake up really early to make things right and do your job. This is actually related to the first disadvantage. Focusing on your job is the key here. Focus on your job, and do not think about going back to sleep until you are done. Remove everything on your table that reminds you of sleeping or any other thing that might distract you, or you'll end up not being able to do your job without getting distracted. Stay focused. But also, don't forget, sleep is also important, don't get sleep deprived, or you won't be able to give your best. If you sleep at 1 A.M. and get up at 5 A.M. and try to do your work, I am sorry, but that will never work; you have to have a sleep schedule on the days when you have to wake up early. You have to shape your life around your job; even though you don't have an office or working hours, you still have a job to do. Remind yourself of this and prepare yourself for the worst.

The third and the most annoying thing is your boss. Yes, I've mentioned that you get to choose your boss when it comes to freelancing, but still, when you are new, or you don't have any other jobs to choose from, you sometimes have to choose someone you don't want and do that might end up with working someone really annoying. For example, you take the job from them, they give you the details about how it is supposed to be done and everything, and after you start, they ask for every little detail, and when you send them the project, they start complaining about every single thing you did, thus resulting in you losing your desire to work and focus on the job. Another example is if they make some kind of shitty excuse about the job and want it early than the deadline that was said. There is actually nothing to do or say about these kinds of stuff because you choose them if you don't have any other choice or you accidentally choose them thinking they won't cause any problem, but they do so, my suggestion is that talk with the people worked before him or maybe search for him online, if he is really good or really bad, something will definitely come up. Use the internet as you do on your job.

One more bad thing is that you do not have a job guarantee every month. I mean, one month, you could earn 1,000 bucks a month, but the next month it could be 400-500 bucks. So you are not financially guaranteed, I guess we could say that. But the thing is, it is not like this every time; it can change when you are really good at your job. So, my opinion on being financially safe about this is that do not quit whatever you are making money from until you have a solid and continuous income from freelancing. Although, I think doing freelancing as a side hustle and also keeping your job is a great way to earn a lot of money. That's what I have been doing since I started this, and I will keep going on doing it, but the bad thing about it is that you won't be able to take weekly jobs, mostly if they are on weekdays because you won't have time to do them, but otherwise, blogging, for example, is a great choice as a side hustle job. You choose yourself from the opportunities. You have tons of opportunities which I recommend before starting to check them all. I already mentioned this in the first chapter of the book. Don't rush it, just wait. For both things, you are choosing your skill and earning a lot of money from it.

Nothing comes easy, especially if it is about money and education.

I know I have mentioned a lot of disadvantages rather than mentioning lots of advantages but one of the reasons why I put the disadvantages part to the last and made it longer than the advantages was because I want the people (that means you) to know the hard things that will come with this job along with its benefits. It's not just about doing the job and getting paid, like everything else in the world; this has bad parts, too. But if we really want to achieve in this job, we have to work hard, just like everything else we do. Just because what you do is on the internet or on social media doesn't mean that you won't have to work as hard as other things, or it will be easy than other jobs. There are times when this job is harder than classical 9-5 jobs. So consider this paragraph and the chapter above as a warning because if you can't pass these things through in your first years, you won't be able to achieve anything. You have to have passion and focus, which are the essential things in this business.

Freelancing is a hard thing, do not think otherwise, but it is in your hands to make it easy in this book, I tried to teach you the basics of how to start freelancing and how to make it continuous so that you will have a side hustle or you can do what you like by getting paid. But as I said tons of times before, be aware of both the consequences and the hard things that you have to go through but also don't be afraid to start because fear comes from the unknown, and you have to learn this in order to see if you can do it or not. If you think you can't do it after you start, don't stop; after a while, you will see that you will be able to do it with passion because you are doing what you love, and this is the purest feeling in the world. Just focus on yourself and on your job. That is all that is needed.